W9-BWE-636

A Note about the Author

ELEANOR FARJEON (1881–1965) is considered one of England's most distinguished writers of children's books. The daughter of an actress and a writer, she grew up in a creative, stimulating home that included an 8,000-volume library. She loved books and was a precocious reader: by age nine she was enjoying Shakespeare.

Her love of reading led quite naturally — and early — to writing. By age seven she was writing poems and stories; by age sixteen she had written the text of an opera produced by the Royal Academy of Music.

She devoted her life to reading and to writing scores of books, many of them for children. During her career she won several major awards, including the Carnegie Medal and the first Hans Christian Andersen Award.

Farjeon originally wrote "Morning Has Broken" for a hymnbook entitled SONGS OF PRAISE, published in 1931. She later included it in one of her collections of poems entitled THE CHILDREN'S BELLS. Although she grew up with no formal religious training, she frequently touched on religious themes in her work. And although she became a member of the Catholic Church rather late in life — in 1951, at the age of seventy — she thought of that step not so much as a conversion but as "a progression to a form of faith towards which my own sense of spiritual life has been moving for the last thirty or forty years."

"Morning Has Broken" is a joyful expression of that growing faith.

Morning Has Broken

BY **Eleanor Farjeon**

ILLUSTRATED BY **Tim Ladwig**

William B. Eerdmans Publishing Company

Grand Rapids, Michigan   Cambridge, U.K.

Copyright © 1996 Wm. B. Eerdmans Publishing Co.

255 Jefferson Ave. S.E., Grand Rapids, Michigan 49503

P.O. Box 163, Cambridge CB3 9PU U.K.

Printed in Hong Kong

00 99 98 97 96   7 6 5 4 3 2 1

The words of "Morning Has Broken" are used by permission of David
Higham Associates, Ltd., London. The music ("Bunessan") is from the
REVISED CHURCH HYMNARY 1927, used by permission of Oxford
University Press.

Library of Congress Cataloging-in-Publication Data
Farjeon, Eleanor, 1881 - 1965.
Morning has broken / by Eleanor Farjeon ; illustrated by Tim Ladwig.
p.   cm.
Summary: An illustrated version of the song which celebrates the beauty
and elation of the newly breaking morning.
ISBN 0-8028-5127-4 (cloth: alk. paper)
ISBN 0-8028-5132-0 (pbk. : alk. paper)
1. Children's songs — Texts.   [1. Morning — Songs and music.
2. Songs.]   I. Ladwig, Tim, ill.   II. Title.
PZ8.3.F228Mh   1996
782.42164'0268 — dc20   96 - 935
[E]   CIP
                                          AC

Book design by Joy Chu

15.00 6/9/03 B&T (8.66)

Morning has broken
like the first morning,

Blackbird has spoken
like the first bird.

Praise for the singing!
Praise for the morning!

Praise for them,
springing
fresh from the Word!

Sweet the rain's new fall
sunlit from heaven,

Like the first dew fall
on the first grass.

Praise for the sweetness of the wet garden,

Sprung in completeness
where His feet pass.

Mine is the sunlight!
Mine is the morning

Born of the one light
Eden saw play!

**Praise with elation,
praise every morning,**

God's re-creation
of the new day!

Morning Has Broken

This is the day that the Lord hath made; we shall rejoice . . . . —Psalm 118:24

Words by Eleanor Farjeon
BUNESSAN traditional Gaelic Melody arranged by David Evans

1 Morn-ing has bro - ken Like the first morn - ing,
2 Sweet the rain's new fall Sun - lit from heav - en,
3 Mine is the sun - light! Mine is the morn - ing

1 Black-bird has spo - ken Like the first bird.
2 Like the first dew - fall On the first grass.
3 Born of the one light E - den saw play!

1 Praise for the sing - ing! Praise for the morn - ing!
2 Praise for the sweet - ness Of the wet gar - den,
3 Praise with e - la - tion, Praise ev - ery morn - ing,

1 Praise for them, spring - ing Fresh from the Word!
2 Sprung in com - plete - ness Where His feet pass.
3 God's re - cre - a - tion Of the new day! A - men.